DK eyewonder
Rocks and Minerals

LONDON, NEW YORK, MELBOURNE,
MUNICH, AND DELHI

Written and edited by Caroline Bingham
Designed by Helen Chapman
Publishing manager Susan Leonard
Managing art editor Clare Shedden
Jacket designer Chris Drew
Picture researcher Sarah Stewart-Richardson
Production Shivani Pandey
DTP designer Almudena Díaz

Consultant Kim Dennis-Bryan PhD, FZS
With thanks to Victoria Long for design assistance.

REVISED EDITION
DK UK
Senior editor Caroline Stamps
Senior art editor Rachael Grady
US editor Margaret Parrish
Jacket editor Manisha Majithia
Jacket designer Natasha Rees
Jacket design development manager
Sophia M Tampakopoulos Turner
Producer (print production) Mary Slater
Producers (pre-production)
Francesca Wardell, Rachel Ng
Publisher Andrew Macintyre

DK INDIA
Senior art editor Rajnish Kashyap
Editor Esha Banerjee
Art editor Isha Nagar
Managing editor Alka Thakur Hazarika
Managing art editor Romi Chakraborty
DTP designer Anita Yadav
Picture researcher Sumedha Chopra

First American Edition, 2003
This American Edition, 2014
Published in the United States by
DK Publishing
4th floor, 345 Hudson Street
New York, New York 10014
13 14 15 16 17 10 9 8 7 6 5 4 3 2 1
001—195885—02/2014
Copyright © 2003, © 2014 Dorling Kindersley Limited

A catalog record for this book is available
from the Library of Congress.
ISBN 978-1-4654-1559-2

DK books are available at special discounts when purchased in bulk for
sales promotions, premiums, fund-raising, or educational use. For details,
contact: DK Publishing Special Markets, 345 Hudson Street, New York,
New York 10014 or SpecialSales@dk.com.

Color reproduction by Scanhouse, Malaysia
Printed and bound in China by Hung Hing

Discover more at
www.dk.com

Contents

car

telephone

jewelry

clothes

Rocky Earth

Rocks and minerals are important. They make up much of our planet and are mined to provide many of the things around us, from cars to computers. Even your body contains minerals that keep you alive.

toothpaste

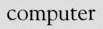
computer

house

you and me!

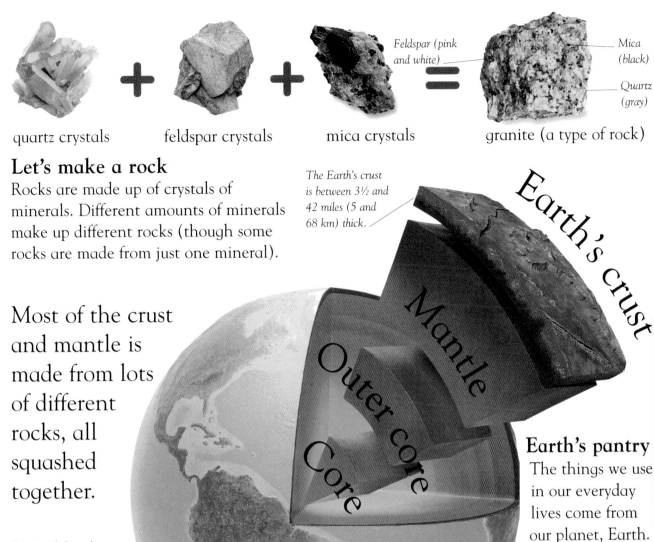

quartz crystals + feldspar crystals + mica crystals = granite (a type of rock)

Feldspar (pink and white)

Mica (black)

Quartz (gray)

Let's make a rock
Rocks are made up of crystals of minerals. Different amounts of minerals make up different rocks (though some rocks are made from just one mineral).

The Earth's crust is between 3½ and 42 miles (5 and 68 km) thick.

Most of the crust and mantle is made from lots of different rocks, all squashed together.

Mantle

Outer core

Core

Earth's crust

Scientists believe the Earth was born about 4.6 billion years ago.

Earth's pantry
The things we use in our everyday lives come from our planet, Earth. The raw ingredients are all taken from the crust. We cannot drill any deeper.

Mineral facts
● Your body contains more than 60 minerals. Nine of these are essential for life.

● Some minerals take thousands of years to form. Some form in minutes.

Let's make shampoo
What forms the shampoo you use on your hair? Minerals, including those below!

coal tar + lithium clay + selenium = shampoo

A volcanic beginning

Squeeze clay in your hands and it oozes between your fingers. This is a little like what happens inside a volcano. The pressure grows until the volcano erupts. Whoosh! It is the first step in the formation of new rocks.

When magma leaves a volcano, it is called lava.

The magma is forced up inside the volcano.

Previous eruptions have formed a cone-shaped exterior.

Magma (molten rock) chamber

No place for a rock?

Deep, deep under the Earth's crust, it is hot enough to melt rock. This molten rock sometimes builds up in chambers and bursts through weak spots in the Earth's crust.

Avalanche of rock

A volcano erupts with such power that sometimes the eruption destroys a part of the volcano. Huge rocks shoot into the air.

Volcanic debris ranges from dust and ash to rocks the size of houses.

Shiprock Pinnacle in New Mexico was once a plug of magma filling the chimney vent of a volcano.

Shiprock Pinnacle is named after a ship because it looks a bit like one.

Just a cliff?

The eruption of a volcano can create deep layers of ash, dust, and rock at its base. It changes the landscape.

Shiprock

Shiprock Pinnacle is all that remains of an ancient volcano. It is the hardened core.

Making of a rock

Do you think that all rocks look alike? In fact, there are many different kinds of rock, but they can be divided into three basic types, all of which are being formed (and destroyed) as you read this book.

In the beginning

The Earth's first rocks were igneous rocks. These form from molten rock that has cooled and hardened.

Molten volcanic rock cools to form igneous rock.

Chipping away

One way sedimentary rock forms is when pieces of rock are carried to the sea, where they create huge piles of sediment. After thousands of years, these cement together.

Sedimentary rock

Sediments are

Sediment settles on the bottom of seas, rivers, and lakes.

builds up in layers.

quashed together.

Getting hotter

Metamorphic rock forms when rocks are transformed as a result of being squeezed and heated deep under the Earth's crust.

The pressure and heat as granite is forced up causes the development of the metamorphic rock marble.

Granite

Deep underground, rocks are being squashed and heated.

Marble

ROCKING AROUND

Over thousands of years, each type of rock can change into one of the others, depending on what happens to it, from igneous to sedimentary to metamorphic.

Igneous rock

Igneous rocks form the greatest part of the Earth's rocky crust, but can also be seen in the land around us. A famous igneous rock landscape is the Giant's Causeway in Northern Ireland.

Pele's hair looks like hair! It forms from sprays of lava.

Pumice stone is the only floating rock.

Pumice is an igneous rock from the heart of a volcano.

Obsidian has a shiny surface. It contains a lot of glass.

From hair to glass

A volcano produces a great variety of igneous rocks. Just take a look at the three examples shown above.

London's Tower Bridge is made of granite.

Built to last

The most common igneous rock is granite. It is incredibly strong and has been used for building for thousands of years.

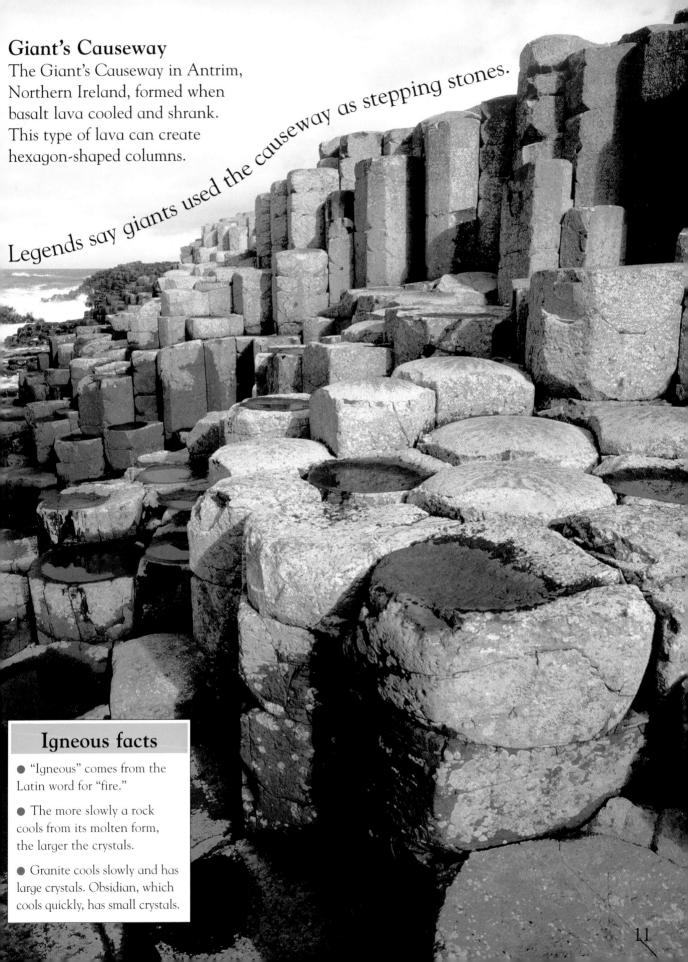

Giant's Causeway

The Giant's Causeway in Antrim, Northern Ireland, formed when basalt lava cooled and shrank. This type of lava can create hexagon-shaped columns.

Legends say giants used the causeway as stepping stones.

Igneous facts

● "Igneous" comes from the Latin word for "fire."

● The more slowly a rock cools from its molten form, the larger the crystals.

● Granite cools slowly and has large crystals. Obsidian, which cools quickly, has small crystals.

Sedimentary rock

Towering chalk cliffs are an amazing example of sedimentary rock. They are formed from the shells and skeletons of microscopic sea creatures. Just imagine how many are needed to build a cliff.

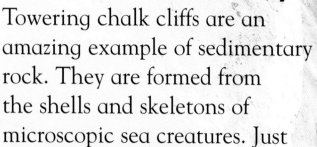

In places, these cliffs are 300 ft (90 m) high.

One by one

The sea creatures that break down to create chalk are tiny. It is thought that these cliffs grew by 0.02 in (0.5 mm) a year—that's about 180 of these creatures piled on top of one another.

Movements in the Earth's crust have lifted the cliffs out of the sea.

From plant to rock

Another way in which sedimentary rocks form is by the breakdown of plants. As these plants are buried, they are squeezed together, eventually forming coal.

Year 1...

From plant matter...

to peat...

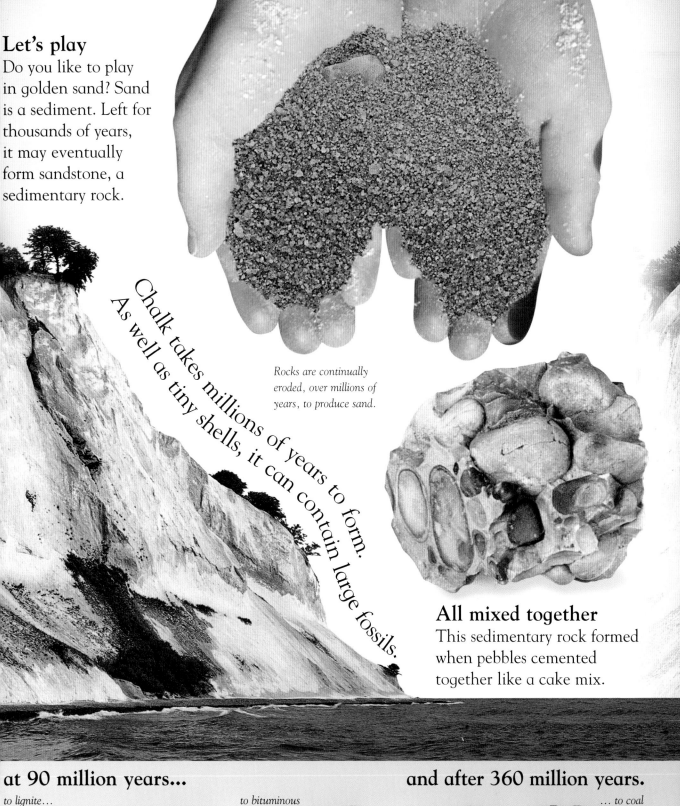

Let's play

Do you like to play in golden sand? Sand is a sediment. Left for thousands of years, it may eventually form sandstone, a sedimentary rock.

Rocks are continually eroded, over millions of years, to produce sand.

Chalk takes millions of years to form. As well as tiny shells, it can contain large fossils.

All mixed together

This sedimentary rock formed when pebbles cemented together like a cake mix.

at 90 million years...

to lignite…

and after 360 million years.

to bituminous coal…

… to coal

Metamorphic rock

"Metamorphic" comes from the ancient Greek words *meta* (meaning "change") and *morphe* (meaning "form"). When rocks are heated or compressed, this type of rock forms.

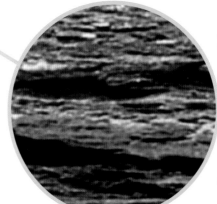

Underground changes
One way metamorphic rocks form is when mountains are pushed up out of the Earth's crust. Mountains and hills surround this old slate quarry.

A peek at slate
The metamorphic rock slate forms from mud and a rock called shale. The shale has been squeezed and compressed as mountains are pushed up. Slate splits easily into sheets.

Each block weighs thousands of tons.

Marble can be carved into statues.

Marble magic
Marble is a beautiful metamorphic rock. It is mined by being cut into huge blocks with strong cutting wires.

Ice-cream swirls

When rocks are heated, parts may begin to melt and run through a "host" rock. This makes swirly patterned metamorphic rock. The rock is called migmatite.

A shimmering palace

Polished marble looks stunning when used for building, and perhaps the world's most famous marble building is the Taj Mahal in India. The marble shimmers in the sun.

The dark host rock contains swirls of a lighter-colored rock.

Marble is formed from limestone.

Water cools the cutting equipment in a quarry.

Rocks from space

We cannot see it, but about 30 tons (25 metric tonnes) of dust rain down on the Earth every day. This fine dust arrives from space. Occasionally, a rock from space hits the Earth; this is called a meteorite.

A meteorite hit

Meteorites are pieces of rock or metal that hit the Earth. Some have broken off asteroids, large chunks of rock that orbit the Sun between Mars and Jupiter. Most are fragments of comets.

There is evidence that a massive meteorite hit the Earth 65 million years ago, causing the dinosaurs to die out.

Meteorites hit the Earth. Meteors burn up above it. Comets pass on by.

What's inside?

Meteorites from asteroids contain metals such as iron, as well as rocks. Those from comets contain more rock than metal.

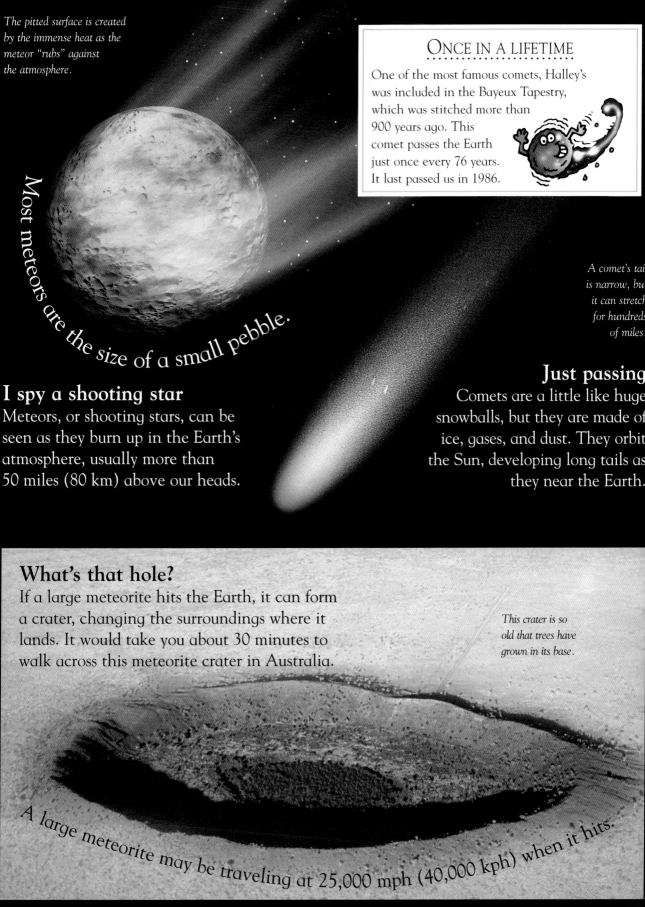

The pitted surface is created by the immense heat as the meteor "rubs" against the atmosphere.

Most meteors are the size of a small pebble.

A comet's tail is narrow, but it can stretch for hundreds of miles.

I spy a shooting star

Meteors, or shooting stars, can be seen as they burn up in the Earth's atmosphere, usually more than 50 miles (80 km) above our heads.

Just passing

Comets are a little like huge snowballs, but they are made of ice, gases, and dust. They orbit the Sun, developing long tails as they near the Earth.

What's that hole?

If a large meteorite hits the Earth, it can form a crater, changing the surroundings where it lands. It would take you about 30 minutes to walk across this meteorite crater in Australia.

This crater is so old that trees have grown in its base.

A large meteorite may be traveling at 25,000 mph (40,000 kph) when it hits.

Hidden beauty

Brrrr! A cave is a damp, dark, chilly place. However, if you are lucky enough to visit a large cave that has been lit and opened to visitors, you'll discover incredibly beautiful shapes in the rocks.

This stream falls farther than the length of a football field.

This cave opens into a vast cavern.

Water damage
Over the course of thousands of years, a constant flow of water will eat away at a solid area of rock. After 100,000 years, this may have formed a small cave, which will continue to grow.

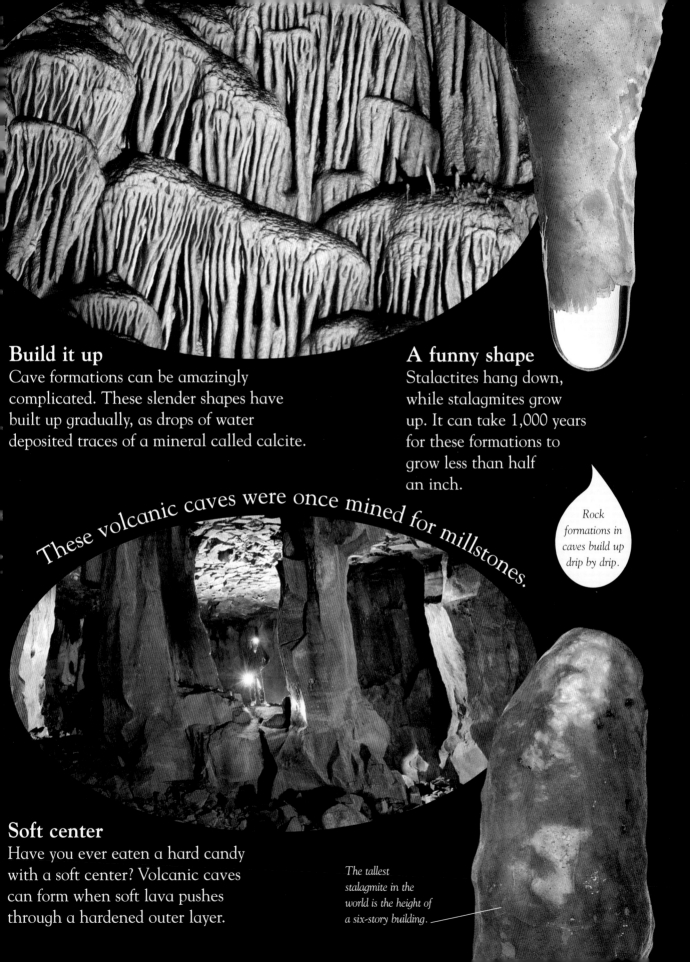

Build it up

Cave formations can be amazingly complicated. These slender shapes have built up gradually, as drops of water deposited traces of a mineral called calcite.

A funny shape

Stalactites hang down, while stalagmites grow up. It can take 1,000 years for these formations to grow less than half an inch.

Rock formations in caves build up drip by drip.

These volcanic caves were once mined for millstones.

Soft center

Have you ever eaten a hard candy with a soft center? Volcanic caves can form when soft lava pushes through a hardened outer layer.

The tallest stalagmite in the world is the height of a six-story building.

Breakdown

Rocks are not as permanent as you might think. From driving rain to frothy seas, when rocks are exposed to wind, water, glaciers, or shifts in temperature, changes begin to happen.

The layers that make up the sedimentary rock in these hoodoos can be clearly seen.

Attack by sea

A long time ago, these stacks were a part of Australia's coastline, but they have been cut off from the coast after constant battering from the sea.

The surrounding rock has been washed away.

Attack by wind and water

Hoodoos are columns of soft sandstone topped by harder rock caps. The cap has protected the rock beneath it from being washed away by heavy downpours of rain.

Attack by river

Over millions of years, the Colorado River has carved its way down into the Grand Canyon, exposing rock faces 6,000 ft (1,830 m) deep.

Attack by acid rain

Pollution from cars and trucks attacks rock. The gases are carried in rainwater to make acids that eat into rock—as shown by the damage to this sculpture.

Hoodoos form spectacular shapes, all clustered together.

If a hoodoo loses its protective cap, the structure will soon begin to wear away.

Erosion creates sediment.

Erosion facts

● The wearing away of a landscape is known as erosion.

● Plants add to rock erosion as their roots burrow their way into cracks in rocks.

● When rocks are broken down where they stand, it is known as weathering.

The force of a glacier is enough to crumble rock.

Carving a path

A glacier is a huge mass of slow-moving ice. Created as snow builds up at the top of a mountain, it begins to force its way forward, picking up rocks and boulders as it moves.

Slow progress
Glaciers usually creep just an inch or two each day. They end lower down the mountain, where the water melts away, or at the coast, where large blocks break off.

Adding the stripes

As a glacier works its way forward, it picks up all kinds of rocks and sediment. This forms darker streaks on the surface of the glacier.

A glacier carves a deep valley as it moves forward.

From rock to flour!

The sides and base of a glacial valley are covered with plenty of scrapes and scratches. This scraping produces fine grains of rock, known as rock flour.

Rock flour is carried down the glacier. Some is deposited in mountain lakes.

Sprinkle on the color!

Mountain lakes are often incredible shades of turquoise blue. This is because of the rock flour fed into them by a melting glacier.

Tiny particles of rock in the water catch the light in a certain way.

Crystals

Have you ever cut a paper snowflake? Snowflakes are made from small ice crystals that collide and stick together. Crystals also form in rock and can be cut and polished.

Beautiful colors

Many crystals come in a rich range of colors. This purple amethyst is a form of quartz. It can also be lilac or mauve.

From little to big

The tiny crystals that make up the endless golden sands of a desert are made of quartz. Quartz can also form gigantic crystals. The largest known rock crystal was about 20 ft (6 m) long!

Crystals continue to grow as long as the surrounding conditions remain the same.

ROCKSICLES, ANYONE?

The word crystal comes from the Greek word *kyros*, which means "icy cold." The ancient Greeks thought quartz crystals were made of ice that had frozen so hard it could not melt.

Amethyst is prized for its color.

Is it a thread?

Not all rock crystals are hard. This is a crystal called tremolite. It forms flexible strands similar to the fibers in material. But you wouldn't be able to sew with tremolite. It could make you sick.

Strands of tremolite have a silky, translucent look because light passes through the fibers.

Seems a little salty

Salt may not seem like a rock, but it is a crystalline rock. In Bolivia there is even a hotel built from salt bricks, including the chairs and tables!

Salt crystals form when seawater evaporates.

The power to heal?

Some people believe that certain crystals have special powers. Jade is thought to help relaxation, lapis lazuli to help friendships.

Lapis lazuli

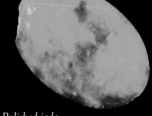

Polished jade

What a gem!

From sparkling diamonds to rich red rubies, some rocks are valuable and are known as gems. They are mined from the Earth at huge expense, cut and polished, and made into jewelry.

Not just a rock
Most gemstones come from rocks. Just imagine if you were lucky enough to find this rock, with its red rubies.

A gem is a stone that has a beautiful color.

Gemstones such as rubies can be rounded and polished, or cut.

Shine on
A cut stone reflects more light, just like this diamond. A cut diamond may have as many as 58 flat sides. Diamond is the hardest mineral of all.

Which are you?
Do you know your birthstone? Some people believe it is lucky to wear a gem that is linked to their month of birth.

January	February	March	April	May

Garnet	Amethyst	Aquamarine	Diamond	Emerald

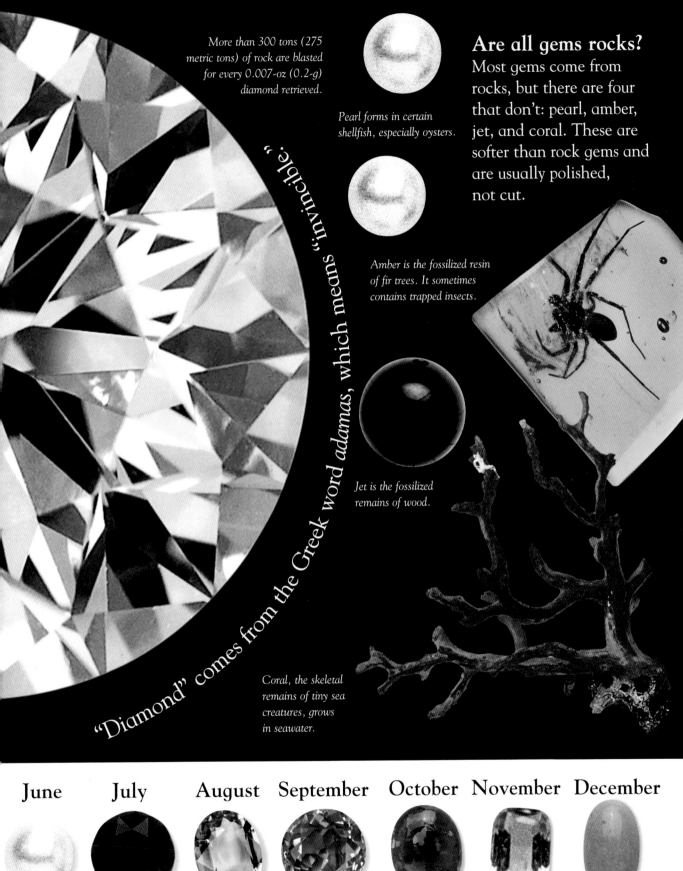

More than 300 tons (275 metric tons) of rock are blasted for every 0.007-oz (0.2-g) diamond retrieved.

Pearl forms in certain shellfish, especially oysters.

Are all gems rocks?

Most gems come from rocks, but there are four that don't: pearl, amber, jet, and coral. These are softer than rock gems and are usually polished, not cut.

Amber is the fossilized resin of fir trees. It sometimes contains trapped insects.

Jet is the fossilized remains of wood.

"Diamond" comes from the Greek word adamas, which means "invincible."

Coral, the skeletal remains of tiny sea creatures, grows in seawater.

June	July	August	September	October	November	December
Pearl	Ruby	Peridot	Sapphire	Opal	Topaz	Turquoise

Precious metals

Gems are not the only treasures hidden deep within our rocky planet. Precious metals such as gold, silver, and platinum have long been mined and used to make objects of great beauty.

Gold is sometimes found in veins of quartz.

Gold

Bangkok, Thailand, is home to the Golden Buddha, a religious statue made of solid gold. It weighs 6 tons (5.5 metric tons)—the weight of a small truck.

Platinum

Platinum is the most expensive metal of all. No wonder it was used to make this crown, part of the British Crown Jewels.

Silver is sometimes found with a delicate frondlike shape.

This rare platinum nugget weighs the same as 10 apples.

Silver

Seven hundred years ago, silver was more valuable than gold. This soft metal was used for coins and jewelry—and for statues such as this Hindu figure.

Get that metal!

Some metals are held inside rocks as minerals—the rock that holds the mineral is known as the ore. Some ores are near the surface, some are deep underground.

Copper pipe
Some of the copper extracted from the mine below will be used to make copper pipes.

Boom!
An open-pit mine is a noisy place. The miners constantly blast away at the rock so they can take it away and extract the metal.

Let's make a hole
Most metals are collected from open-pit mines. This means that the surface is blasted and tons of rock are removed, truckload by truckload.

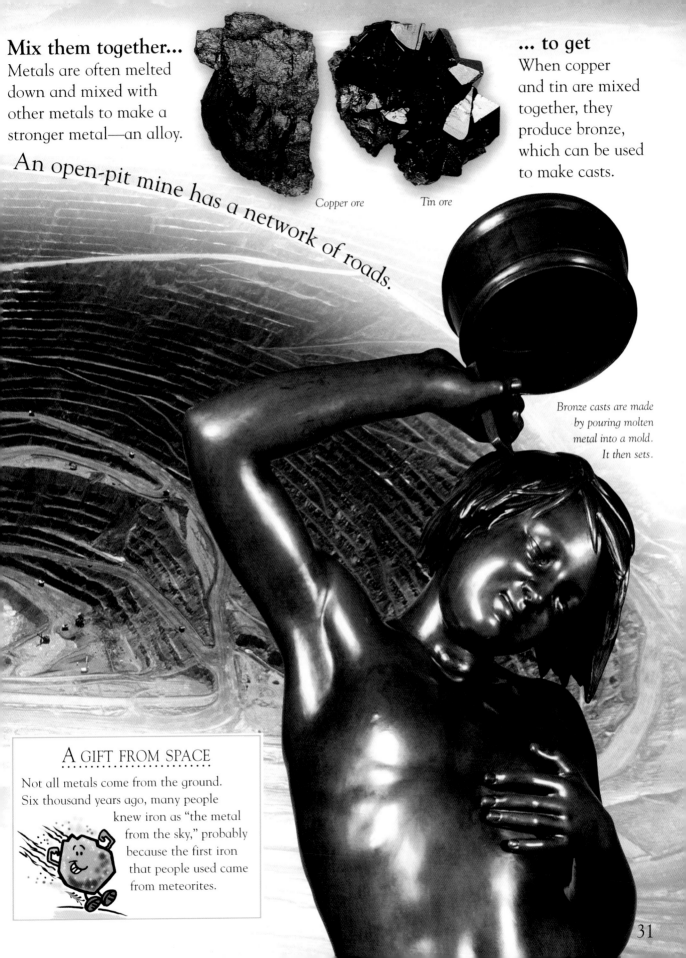

Mix them together...

Metals are often melted down and mixed with other metals to make a stronger metal—an alloy.

Copper ore

Tin ore

... to get

When copper and tin are mixed together, they produce bronze, which can be used to make casts.

An open-pit mine has a network of roads.

Bronze casts are made by pouring molten metal into a mold. It then sets.

A GIFT FROM SPACE

Not all metals come from the ground. Six thousand years ago, many people knew iron as "the metal from the sky," probably because the first iron that people used came from meteorites.

Using rocks in art

Have you ever used a rock to draw? It's lots of fun to use chalk and scribble away on a sidewalk. The colors held inside some rocks and minerals have been used by artists for thousands of years.

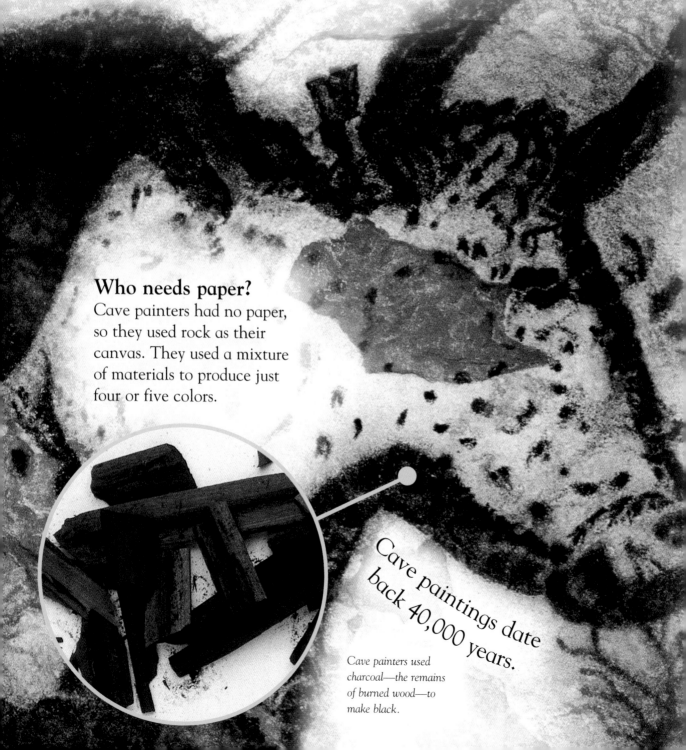

Who needs paper?
Cave painters had no paper, so they used rock as their canvas. They used a mixture of materials to produce just four or five colors.

Cave paintings date back 40,000 years.

Cave painters used charcoal—the remains of burned wood—to make black.

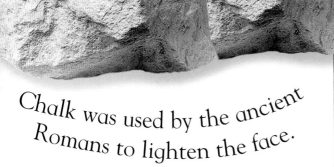

Chalk was used by the ancient Romans to lighten the face.

A light source

The sedimentary rock chalk is messy to use, but it is a fantastic material for showing how light bounces off an object.

Gold was extracted from a mineral and used in this 600-year-old painting.

Cinnabar was first used in ancient China.

Rich reds

The powder of a mineral rock called cinnabar makes a brilliant red that was widely used in religious art in the Middle Ages.

Cinnabar is the main source of the poisonous metal mercury.

Rocks in history

A long time ago, someone somewhere picked up a stone and used it as a tool. It was the beginning of something big, as people found more and more ways in which to use rocks.

Just down the road
In the past, there were no machines to move building materials, so people had to use what was available nearby. These roofs are covered with slate taken from a local quarry.

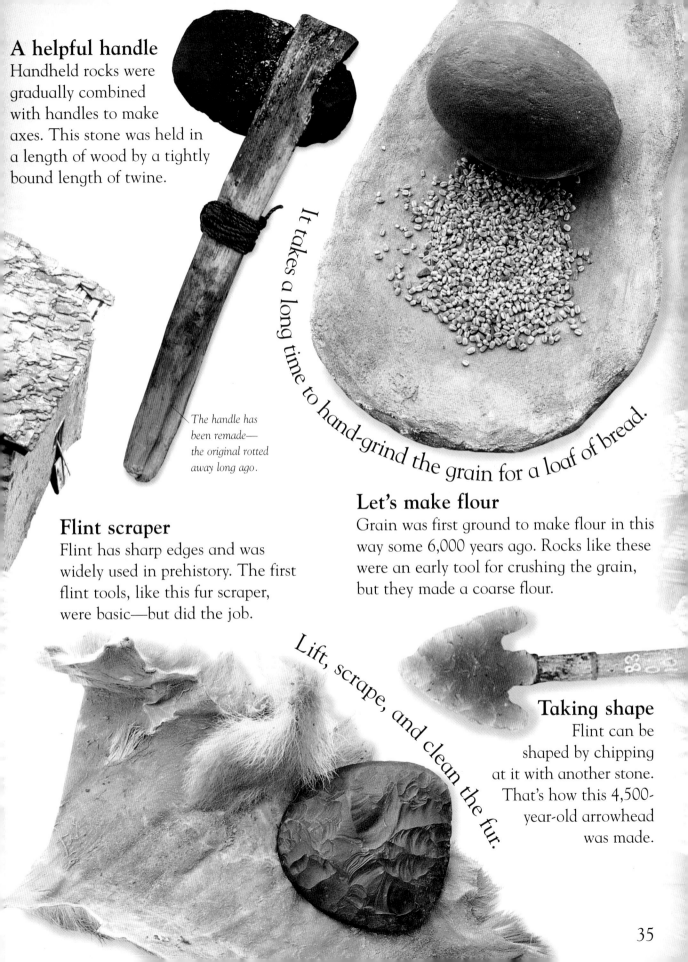

A helpful handle
Handheld rocks were gradually combined with handles to make axes. This stone was held in a length of wood by a tightly bound length of twine.

The handle has been remade—the original rotted away long ago.

It takes a long time to hand-grind the grain for a loaf of bread.

Let's make flour
Grain was first ground to make flour in this way some 6,000 years ago. Rocks like these were an early tool for crushing the grain, but they made a coarse flour.

Flint scraper
Flint has sharp edges and was widely used in prehistory. The first flint tools, like this fur scraper, were basic—but did the job.

Lift, scrape, and clean the fur.

Taking shape
Flint can be shaped by chipping at it with another stone. That's how this 4,500-year-old arrowhead was made.

Building rocks

Take a look around you. Rocks are everywhere—in the sidewalks and the roads, in the houses in which we live, and in the skyscrapers that tower above us. They are the building blocks of modern cities.

From a mold

Bricks are made from clay, which is shaped in molds and fired in huge ovens, called kilns, to bake it.

Skyscrapers

Skyscrapers are built from a variety of manufactured materials on a steel framework. Many of these materials come from rocks that have been mined.

The building's steel framework is strong but also flexible in high winds.

sand + gravel + cement + water = concrete

Rock solid

Mix together the above ingredients and you will make concrete, a building material that quickly sets rock hard. It is used all over the world.

The ancient Romans used concrete for their buildings.

Today, most window glass is coated to strengthen it.

Let in the light

Natural glass is as old as our planet—it forms when lava cools. The first (small) artificial glass sheets were made about 1,000 years ago.

A touch of mystery

Some rocks and minerals look so
unusual that myths and legends
have grown up around them.
From Devil's toenails to
desert roses, the weird
and wonderful are
all around us.

*Wave Rock is
the height of a
three-story house.*

A HISSING STONE?

Snakestones were once believed to be the remains
of coiled snakes turned to stone
by a 7th-century abbess called
St. Hilda. They are actually
ammonites, the fossils of
shelled sea creatures, which
were sometimes given
carved snake heads.

Surf's up

Wave Rock in Australia is well named. This
massive rock is one-and-a-half times the
length of a jumbo jet. It has formed as much
softer rock beneath the upper lip wears away.

Taking root

Is it a tree root, or maybe an animal's burrow? No. This is fulgurite. It forms when lightning strikes sand and fuses the grains.

The forks follow the lightning's path.

Fulgurite is a glassy rock.

Are they toenail clippings?

These rocks were once believed to be the Devil's toenails. In fact, they are fossils—the remains of oyster shells.

Which way?

Magnetite is a magnetic mineral and was used in early compasses. We now use magnetite to produce iron as it contains a lot of iron.

Is it real?

Desert roses look very pretty, but they have no smell. They form in the desert from a mineral called barite.

The streaks are caused by minerals being washed down the rock by downpours of rain.

History in a rock

Rocks hide a lot of things, but perhaps the most exciting are the secrets rocks tell about life on the Earth millions of years ago, when the dinosaurs ruled.

A dead beginning

A dinosaur lies down to die on a sandy shore. Perhaps it will not be eaten, and its skeleton will remain intact as its flesh rots away. The long path to becoming a fossil has begun.

A special scientist called a paleontologist can discover how old a fossil is by

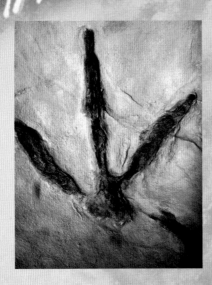

What's that?

Imagine your footsteps being found by some one in the future, preserved forever in rock. Fossil footprints are a curious reminder of creatures long dead.

The fossils that have been discovered are only a tiny percentage of the animals that have lived.

Fossil dinosaur

The skeleton of this dinosaur has been preserved because the animal was covered in mud soon after death and squeezed between layers of sediment.

studying the rocks around it.

Big gnashers

Teeth are one of the most commonly found fossils—they last well because they are so hard. These belonged to a dinosaur called *Iguanodon*.

Clean up time

It takes a long time to extract a large fossil from the rock in which it is encased. The paleontologist working on it does not want to damage it.

The rock and dust surrounding a fossil are removed particle by particle if necessary.

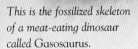

This is the fossilized skeleton of a meat-eating dinosaur called Gasosaurus.

Fossil facts

● The parts of an animal most likely to fossilize are the hard bits: the bones, teeth, or shell.

● Fossils of footprints, or trackways, are called trace fossils.

● Fossils are found in sedimentary rock, such as limestone.

41

Hunting for rocks

Once you begin to learn about rocks and minerals, it's fun to go and look for some interesting rocks yourself. You may find a rock containing a fossil!

The spiral pattern of this long-fossilized ammonite can be seen in the nautilus shells of today.

Leave no stone unturned
This child is looking for fossils. Depending on where in the world you live, you may have to be careful when looking for rocks: in some countries they hide dangerous creatures.

Start your rock collection by hunting for pebbles of different colors.

Mohs scale
Geologists use the Mohs scale, which was set up in 1812, to measure a rock's hardness. The higher the number, the harder the rock.

| **1** | **2** | **3** | **4** |
| Talc | Gypsum | Calcite | Fluorite |

2.5
Fingernail

42

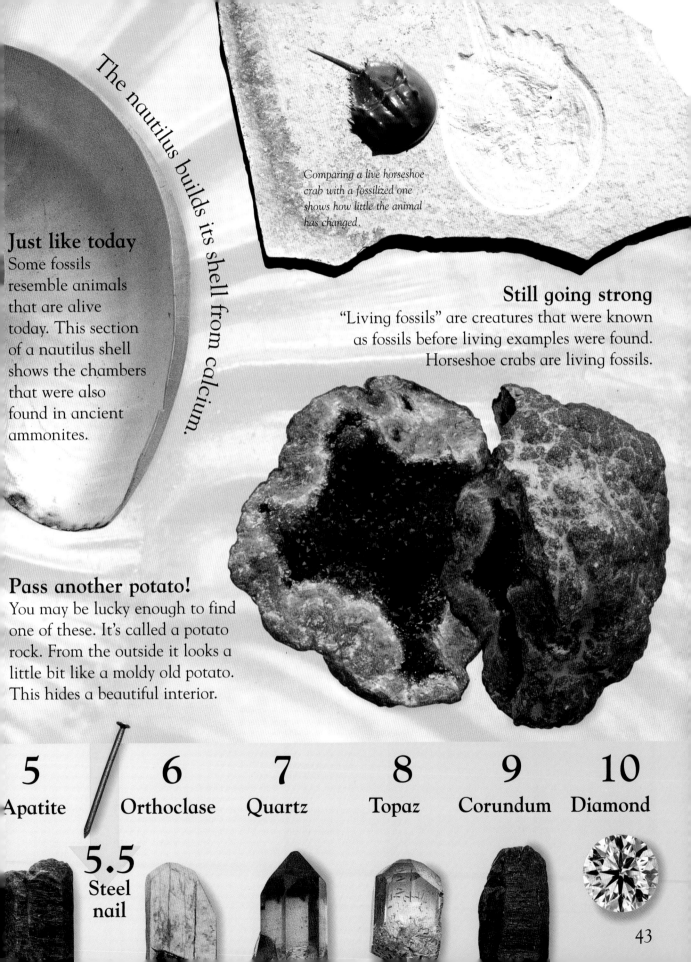

Comparing a live horseshoe crab with a fossilized one shows how little the animal has changed.

Just like today

Some fossils resemble animals that are alive today. This section of a nautilus shell shows the chambers that were also found in ancient ammonites.

Still going strong

"Living fossils" are creatures that were known as fossils before living examples were found. Horseshoe crabs are living fossils.

Pass another potato!

You may be lucky enough to find one of these. It's called a potato rock. From the outside it looks a little bit like a moldy old potato. This hides a beautiful interior.

5	6	7	8	9	10
Apatite	Orthoclase	Quartz	Topaz	Corundum	Diamond

5.5
Steel nail

43

What does it make?

Rocks and minerals, and the metals that are taken from them, can be found in many of the everyday objects that surround you. Just take a look!

Clay is used in...
books
pencils
pottery

Fluorite is used in...
toothpaste
ceramics
water

Garnet is used in...
sandpaper
glass
jewelry

Limestone is used in...
cleaning products
books
concrete

Quartz is used in...

computers

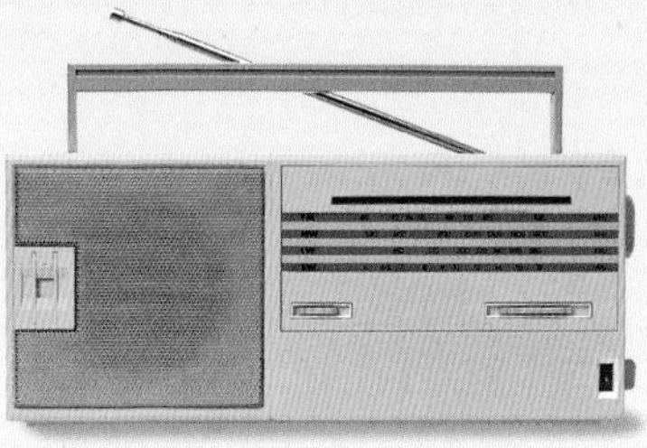

radios

watch batteries

Silica sand is used in...

televisions

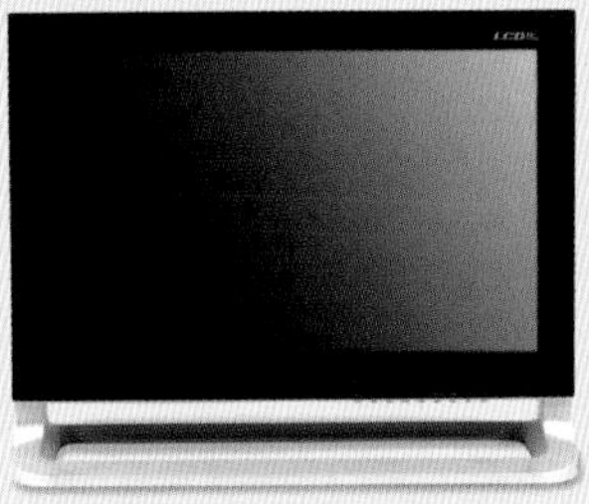

glass

plastic buckets

Silver is used in...

telephones

cameras

picture frames

Sulfur is used in...

film

matches

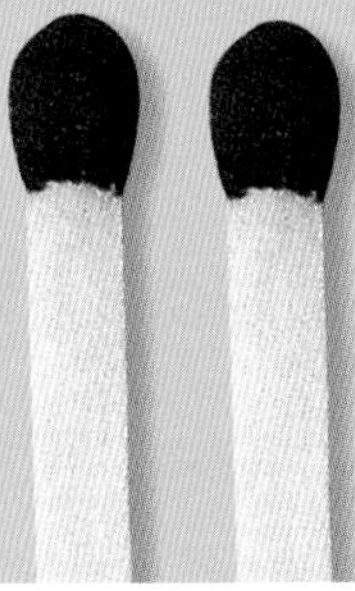

paper

Talc is used in...

paint

ceramics

talcum powder

Precious stones

Rumors tell of a hidden treasure, brimming with precious gems. Will you find it before someone else beats you to it? Good luck!

Catch sight of the treasure. **Move forward 3**

Shelter from a meteorite shower. **Skip a turn**

Stop to mine. **Move back 4**

Trip up over rocks. **Move back 4**

Dynamite clears path. **Roll again**

START

Climb a cliff to continue. **Skip a turn**

FINISH

You have found the precious stones.

How to play

This is a game for up to four players.

You will need
- A die
- Counters—one for each player.

Move down! Move up!

Trace over the gems below or cut and color your own from cardboard. Each player takes a turn rolling the die and begins from the START box. Follow the squares with each roll of the die. If you land on an instruction, make sure you do as it says. Good luck!

Run to avoid lava flow.
Move forward 4

Take a helicopter ride.
Move forward 5

Giant boulders block path.
Go back 5

Dead end.
Go back 4

Pot holes ahead, change route.
Go back 6

Find a tunnel to use as a shortcut.
Move forward 4

True or false?

How much have you learned about rocks and minerals? See if you can spot which of these statements are false.

Gold can be found in veins of quartz.
See page 28

Amethyst is a form of quartz crystal.
See page 24

First used more than 70,000 years ago, hand axes had wooden handles.
See page 34

By mixing copper and tin we get bronze, which can be used to make casts.
See page 31

Corals are plants found underwater.
See page 27

If you enter a limestone cave you might find stalagmites hanging from its roof.
See page 19

Chalk is a sedimentary rock that takes millions of years to form.
See page 13

All gems used in jewelry and other precious items come from rocks.
See page 27

Fossils are mostly found on igneous rocks.
See page 41

Some metals are extracted from rocks. These rocks are known as ores.
See page 30

Rocks are permanent by nature and stay unaffected by natural forces.
See page 20

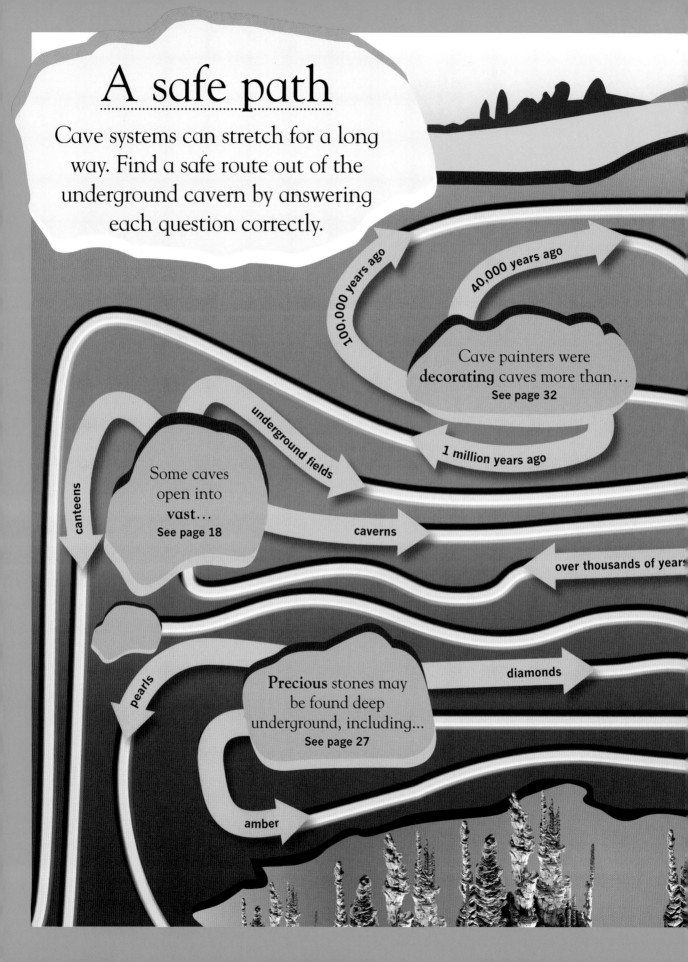

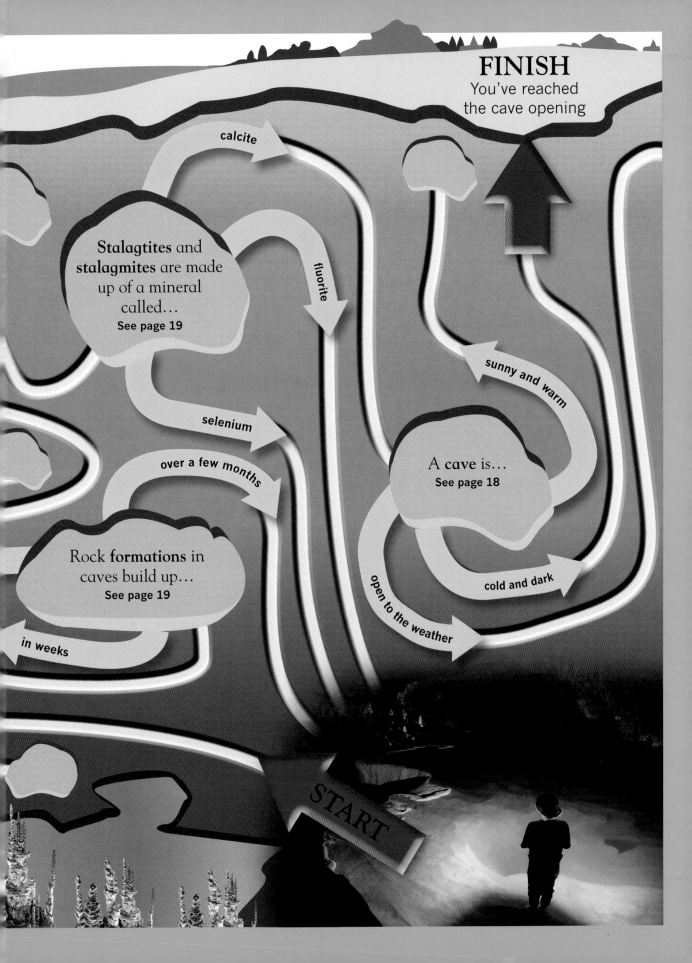

Facts match

Rocks and minerals are found everywhere. Read the clues and see if you can match them with the correct images.

Pearls

Horseshoe crab

Magnetite

Cinnabar

Diamond

Flint

Hoodoo

We use this white crystalline rock almost every day. See page 25

This was used by early man 40,000 years ago to make paintings on the walls of caves. See page 32

This rose-shaped rock is made up of the mineral barite. See page 39

This sea creature is also called a living fossil. See page 43

This rock gets formed when parts of rocks melt and mix to form patterns that may resemble an ice-cream swirl. See page 15

This mineral was used in early compasses. It is now used to produce iron. See page 39

This mineral was commonly used in art during the Middle Ages. See page 33

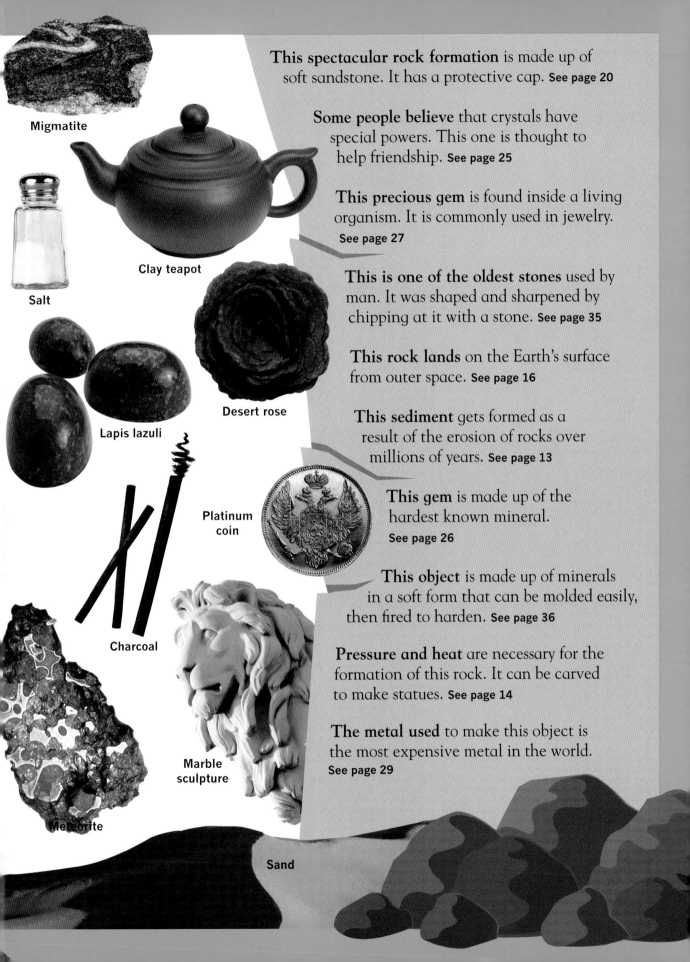

Migmatite

Salt

Clay teapot

Lapis lazuli

Desert rose

Platinum coin

Charcoal

Marble sculpture

Meteorite

Sand

This spectacular rock formation is made up of soft sandstone. It has a protective cap. **See page 20**

Some people believe that crystals have special powers. This one is thought to help friendship. **See page 25**

This precious gem is found inside a living organism. It is commonly used in jewelry. **See page 27**

This is one of the oldest stones used by man. It was shaped and sharpened by chipping at it with a stone. **See page 35**

This rock lands on the Earth's surface from outer space. **See page 16**

This sediment gets formed as a result of the erosion of rocks over millions of years. **See page 13**

This gem is made up of the hardest known mineral. **See page 26**

This object is made up of minerals in a soft form that can be molded easily, then fired to harden. **See page 36**

Pressure and heat are necessary for the formation of this rock. It can be carved to make statues. **See page 14**

The metal used to make this object is the most expensive metal in the world. **See page 29**

Glossary

Here are the meanings of some words that are useful
to know when learning about rocks and minerals.

Alloy a metal that is made by combining two or more metals.

Basalt one of the most common forms of igneous rock.

Coal a rock made from plants that have been buried and squeezed over millions of years.

Crystal a naturally occurring substance with a specific makeup that forms particular types of minerals.

Erosion the wearing away of a landscape.

Fossil the preserved remains of ancient life or evidence of their activity.

Glacier a mass of ice or snow that flows under its own weight.

Igneous rock rock made from molten rock that has cooled and hardened.

Hoodoo a column of soft rock with a harder lid that protects it from erosion.

Lava the molten rock (magma) that has erupted from a volcano.

Lignite a woody kind of rock made from plants before they become coal.

Magma molten rock found deep inside the Earth.

Mantle the part of the Earth's interior that lies between the crust and the core.

Metamorphic rock rock melted by heat and pressure that cools and recrystallizes in a different form.

Meteor a lump of rock or metal from outer space that burns up as it enters the Earth's atmosphere.

Meteorite a meteor that has fallen to Earth.

Mineral a naturally occurring substance with very specific characteristics, such as hardness.

Nugget a small piece of something valuable, like gold.

Open-pit mine a mine with an open top instead of tunnels under the Earth's surface.

Ore a rock that holds minerals.

Quarry a place where stone is dug up.

Sediment pieces of rock and plant and animal material that are carried by water, wind, or ice and are usually deposited some way from their origin.

Sedimentary rock rock that is formed when small pieces of rock or plant and animal remains become stuck together.

Weathering the breakdown of rock by the weather.

Index

Acknowledgements

Dorling Kindersley would like to thank:
Dorian Spencer Davies for original artwork, Fleur Star for help with the glossary, and Pilar Morales for DTP assistance.

Picture credits

The publisher would like to thank the following for their kind permission to reproduce their photographs: (Key: a-above; b-below/bottom; c-center; f-far; l-left; r-right; t-top)

1 Corbis: David Forman/Eye Ubiquitous; 2-3 Corbis: Durrell Gulin; 4tl Dreamstime.com: Supertrooper; 4bl Daniele Taurino; 5tr & tcr Dorling Kindersley: National History Museum, London, 5bl & bcl GeoScience Features Picture Library; 5bcr Corbis: Lester V Bergman; 6t Getty Images: Schafer & Hill; 7tl Science Photo Library: Stephen & Donna O'Meara; 8bl Corbis: James A.Sugar; 8-9c Getty Images: Spencer Jones; 8-9b SPL: Bill Bachman; 9t Corbis: Galen Rowell; 9tl & cl Dorling Kindersley: National History Museum, London; 9c & b Corbis: M. Angelo; 10bl Corbis: Martin Jones; 10br GeoScience Features Picture Library; 11 Corbis: Ric Ergenbright; 11tcr Dorling Kindersley: National History Museum, 12-13 Ardea London Ltd: Ake Lindau; 12c Ardea London Ltd: P.Morris; 12 bl & br Dorling Kindersley: National History Museum, London; 13c, bl, bc & br Dorling Kindersley: National History Museum, London; 14-15 Corbis: WildCountry; 14tl Corbis: Richard Klune; 14tr GeoScience Features Picture Library, 14b Corbis: Araldode Luca; 16-17 Science Photo Library: Mike Agliolo, 16r Science Photo Library: Detlev Van Ravensswaay, 17c Science Photo Library: Eckhard Slawik,17t Science Photo Library: Mehau Kulyk, 17b Science Photo Library: Bill Bachman; 18 Corbis: Annie Griffiths Belt; 18tl Dorling Kindersley: National History Museum, London; 19t Corbis: Craig Lovell; 19b Corbis: Roger Ressmeyer, 20-21 Science Photo Library: David Nunuk; 20r Corbis: Royalty-Free; 22-23 Science Photo Library: Bernhard Edmaier, 22t Science Photo Library: Simon Fraser, 23c Ardea London Ltd: Francois Gohier, 24 Science Photo Library: Sinclair Stammers; 25t Dorling Kindersley: National History Museum, London; 25cr SPL: Cristina Pedrazzini, 25 bl & br Science Photo Library:

Vaughan Fleming, 26-27 & 26bcr Science Photo Library: Alfred Pasieka; 26-27c Dreamstime.com: Mishatc, 26br Dreamstime.com: Mishatc, 26tl Science Photo Library: J.C.Revy, 26c Science Photo Library: Lawrence Lawry, 26bl Dorling Kindersley: National History Museum, London; 27tr, crb, br, bcr & brl Dorling Kindersley: National History Museum, London; 28-29 Corbis: Lindsay Hebberd, 28l Corbis: ML Sinibaldi, 29r Corbis: Tim Graham, 30-31 Corbis: Yann Arthus-Bertrand; 30b Getty Images: Jaime Villaseca; 31bl Dorling Kindersley: National History Museum, London; 31b Corbis: The State Russian Museum, 32 Corbis Sygma: Pierre Vauthey; 33tr Dorling Kindersley Picture Library: Museo de Zaragoza; 33c Dorling Kindersley Picture Library: Museum of London; 33bl Corbis: David Lees, 34 Corbis: Ric Ergenbright, 35tr & bl Dorling Kindersley Picture Library: Museum of London, 35br Dorling Kindersley Picture Library: British Museum; 36-37 Corbis: Lee White; 37tl Dorling Kindersley: National History Museum, London; 37cb Corbis: Michael Prince; 38-39 Ardea London Ltd: Jean-Paul Ferrero; 39tl Science Photo Library: Astrid & Hanns-Frieder; 39tr Science Photo Library: Peter Menzel; 39cl Dorling Kindersley: National History Museum, London; 39br SPL: Martin Land, 40-41 Science Photo Library: Mehau Kulyk; 40tl Dorling Kindersley: National History Museum, London; 40bc SPL: Sinclair Stammers, 42-43 Science Photo Library: Lawrence Lawry; 42cl Getty Images: Clarissa Leahy; Corbis: Jeffrey L. Rotman; 43bcl Dorling Kindersley: National History Museum, London; 43br Dreamstime.com: Mishatc, 44tr Dorling Kindersley Picture Library: British Museum; 44cr Dreamstime.com: Juan Moyano; 45tl Dorling Kindersley: National History Museum, London; 45ca, tl, c & cr Dreamstime.com: Kitchner Bain, Daniele Taurino, Brett Critchley, Olira; 46cla Corbis: Albert Lleal / Minden Pictures; 46cra Getty Images: Stocktrek; 47bl Dorling Kindersley: Rough Guides; 48l & 49r Science Photo Library: Dr. Jeremy Burgess; 48bl Dreamstime.com: Alexander Khromtsov; 48cl Getty Images: Siede Preis / Photodisc; 49cl Dorling Kindersley: National History Museum, London; 49c Dreamstime.com: Elen; 49b Libux77; 49cr Getty Images: Jaime Villaseca / Stone; 50-51bc Dorling Kindersley: Aven Armand; 51br Corbis: Sean White, Design Pics, Design Pics; 52cra Dorling Kindersley: L. Cornelissen and Son Ltd; 52c National History Museum, London; 52ca, tr, br & cr Dreamstime.com: Kevin Knuth , Pzaxe, Kolaczan; 52cr Fotolia: apttone; 53cb Corbis: James L. Amos; 53ca Dorling Kindersley: National History Museum, London; 53bc Rough Guides; 53tc & cl Dreamstime.com: Alexpurs, Alexander Hoffmann, 54-55 Corbis: Owaki-Kulla.

All other images © Dorling Kindersley.
For further information see: www.dkimages.com

Timothy Tunny Swallowed a Bunny
Text copyright © 2000 by Bill Grossman
Illustrations copyright © 2000 by Kevin Hawkes
Manufactured in China. All rights reserved.
www.harperchildrens.com

Library of Congress Cataloging-in-Publication Data
Grossman, Bill.
Timothy Tunny swallowed a bunny / by Bill Grossman ; illustrated by Kevin Hawkes.
p. cm.
Summary: Presents eighteen whimsical poems about people caught in unusual situations.
ISBN 0-06-028010-7 – ISBN 0-06-028758-6 (lib. bdg.) – ISBN 0-06-051604-6 (pbk.)
1. Children's poetry, American. [1. Nonsense verses. 2. American poetry.] I. Hawkes, Kevin, ill.
II. Title.
PS3557.R6715 T56 2000   99-48093
811'.54–dc21   CIP
                                                                         AC

Typography by Alicia Mikles
❖

TIMOTHY TUNNY SWALLOWED A BUNNY

BY BILL GROSSMAN
ILLUSTRATED BY KEVIN HAWKES

A LAURA GERINGER BOOK
An Imprint of HarperCollins*Publishers*